Copyright © 2020 by Amanda Beth Martin

All rights reserved. No part of this book may be reproduced in any form or by any electronic or mechanical means, including information storage and retrieval systems, without express permission in writing from the publisher. For information regarding permission, write to The Victorian Panda, thevictorianpanda@gmail.com.

ISBN 978-1-7356873-0-8 (Paperback Edition)
ISBN 978-1-7356873-2-2 (Ebook Edition)

Let's Talk Bilingual!
Let's Talk Summer Clothes! / ¡Hablemos de ropa de verano! Amanda Beth Martin

Library of Congress Control Number: 2020917520

First edition: September 2020
Book design by Amanda Beth Martin
Illustrations copyright © by Amanda Beth Martin

Published by The Victorian Panda
www.thevictorianpanda.com
thevictorianpanda@gmail.com

For my Sister.

A special thank you to my Aunt Kathy for illustrating the armoire. Gracias to Fayme, Gerald, Kevin, Jeff, and Sonia for their time and expertise with the translations.

It's summer!

¡Es verano!

In the summer it is hot and sunny outside.

En verano hace calor y afuera está soleado.

What do we wear in the summer?

¿Qué usamos en verano?

Let's look in our armoire!

¡Miremos en nuestro ropero!

Baseball hat

Una gorra de béisbol

Flip flops

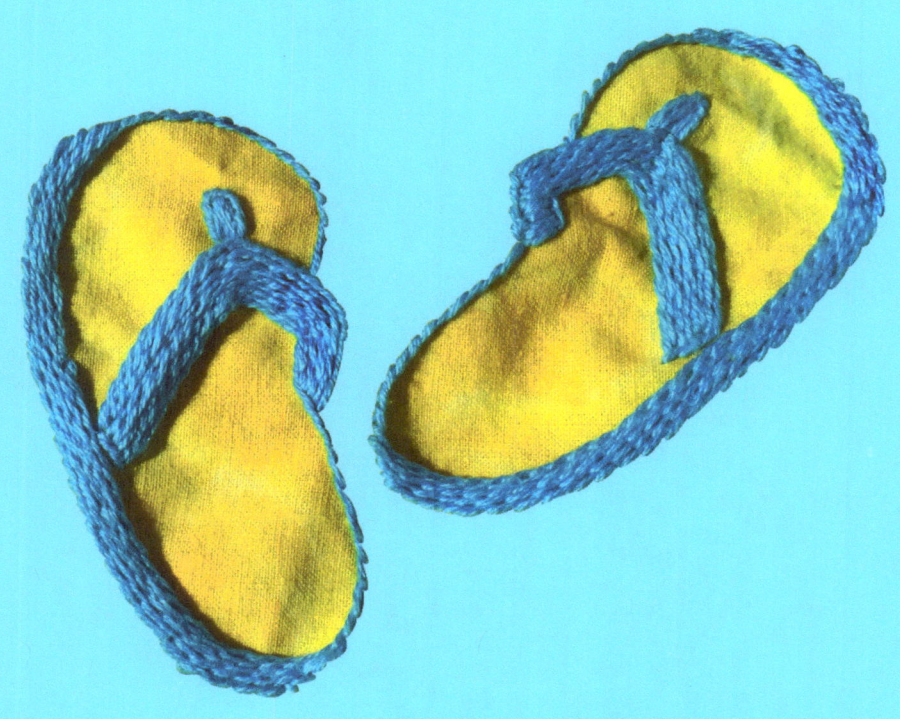

Unas chanclas

Tank top

Una camiseta sin mangas

Swim trunks

Un traje de baño para hombre

Swimsuit

Un traje de baño para mujer

Sundress

Un vestido de sol

Sunglasses

Unos lentes de sol

T-shirt

Una playera

Shorts

Unos pantalones cortos

Sandals

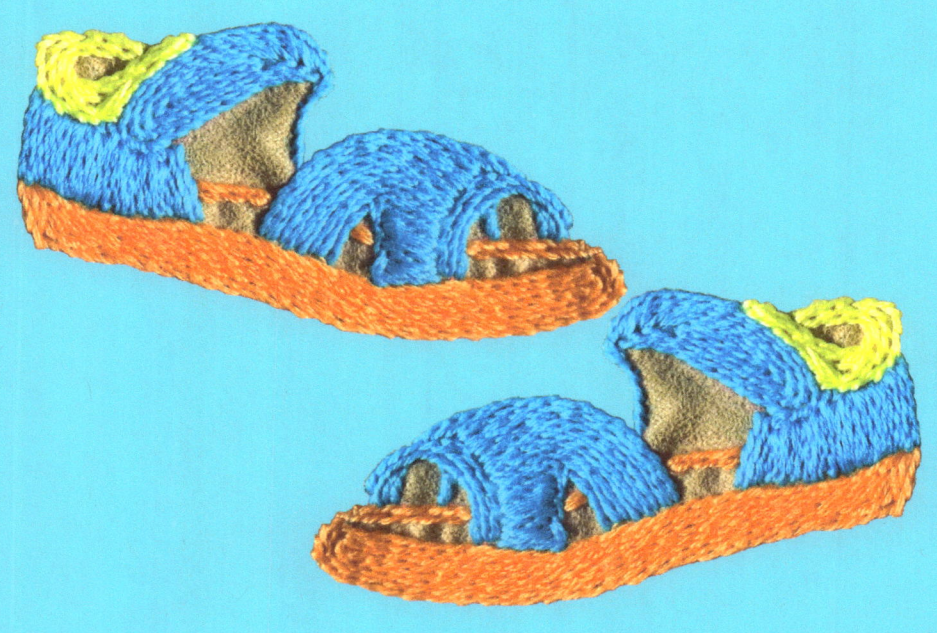

Unas sandalias

Sun hat

Un sombrero para el sol

What are your favorite summer clothes?

¿Cuál es tu ropa de verano favorita?

www.ingramcontent.com/pod-product-compliance
Lightning Source LLC
Chambersburg PA
CBHW042256100526
44589CB00002B/47